Donald Trump

by Grace Hansen

ABDO
UNITED STATES
PRESIDENT BIOGRAPHIES
Kids

abdopublishing.com

Published by Abdo Kids, a division of ABDO, PO Box 398166, Minneapolis, Minnesota 55439.

Copyright © 2017 by Abdo Consulting Group, Inc. International copyrights reserved in all countries. No part of this book may be reproduced in any form without written permission from the publisher.

Printed in the United States of America, North Mankato, Minnesota.

102016

012017

THIS BOOK CONTAINS RECYCLED MATERIALS

Photo Credits: Alamy, AP Images, Getty Images, iStock, Shutterstock, Thinkstock, ©Carrienelson1 p.Cover / Dreamstime.com, ©Seth Poppel p.7,9 / Yearbook Library, ©stock_photo_world p.17 / Shutterstock.com

Production Contributors: Teddy Borth, Jennie Forsberg, Grace Hansen

Design Contributors: Laura Mitchell, Dorothy Toth

Publisher's Cataloging-in-Publication Data

Names: Hansen, Grace, author.

Title: Donald Trump / by Grace Hansen.

Description: Minneapolis, MN : Abdo Kids, 2017 | Series: United States president biographies | Includes bibliographical references and index.

Identifiers: LCCN 2016944101 | ISBN 9781680809398 (lib. bdg.) | ISBN 9781680796490 (ebook) | ISBN 9781680797169 (Read-to-me ebook)

Subjects: LCSH: Trump, Donald, 1946- --Juvenile literature. | Presidents--United States--Biography--Election, 2016--Juvenile literature.

Classification: DDC 973.929/092 [B]--dc23

LC record available at http://lccn.loc.gov/2016944101

Table of Contents

Early Years

Donald John Trump was born on June 14, 1946. He was raised in Queens, New York.

New York

Donald was one of five children. He was **bold** and full of energy. His parents had to steer him in the right direction. They sent him to a military high school.

Soon, Donald was a student leader and a top athlete. He graduated in 1964. He later enrolled at Wharton School of Finance. He graduated in 1968.

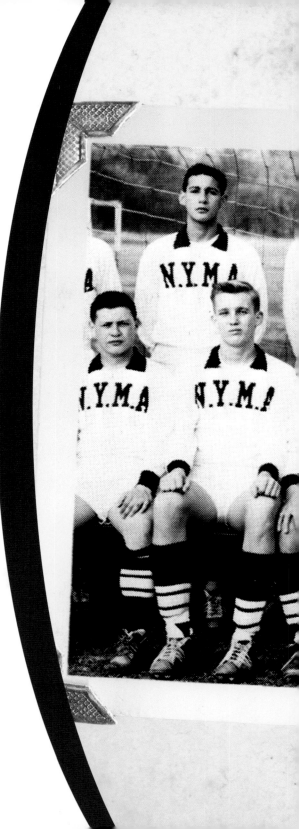

9

Trump joined his father in the real estate business. In 1971, Trump took over his father's company. He renamed it Trump Organization.

11

Family

Trump has five children. Three of them help run his company. He married his wife, Melania, in 2005.

13

Trump was well known in the **real estate** business. But he became a **household name** hosting *The Apprentice*. He also **produced** the series from 2004 to 2015.

In 2015, Trump announced he was running for president. He went up against 16 other **Republican** candidates. He won the **nomination** in July 2016.

Trump for President

Trump ran against Hillary Clinton. The election was close until the very end.

19

November 8, 2016, was a historic day. Trump was elected the 45th US president. With great **ambition**, Trump went from businessman to president in less than 18 months.

More Facts

- Trump has a star on the Hollywood Walk of Fame for his role in NBC's *The Apprentice*.

- Trump considered running for president in 2000.

- Trump is the first United States president with no political or military background.

Glossary

ambition – a strong want to do something.

bold – very confident in a way that might seem rude.

household name – well known by the public.

nomination – the act of formally choosing someone as a candidate for a position.

produced – to oversee all aspects of a television program.

real estate – the business of selling land and buildings.

Republican – a member of the Republican Party, who generally believes in a smaller government role.

Index

abdokids.com

Use this code to log on to abdokids.com and access crafts, games, videos and more!

Abdo Kids Code:
PTK9398